# HAPPINESS

## The Workbook

Robert J. Spitzer, S.J., Ph.D.

# HAPPINESS

## The Workbook

IGNATIUS PRESS     SAN FRANCISCO

Cover design by John Herreid

Cover photograph by Jim Breen

ISBN 978-1-58617-961-8
Printed in the United States of America ∞

# Contents

# Lesson One—The Four Levels of Happiness

## I. Series Introduction: What Happiness Means to You

Episode Timecode
**1:08**

### The Mystery of Unhappiness

What does it take to be happy?

Sometimes people seem to have everything they could ever want, but they are still unhappy. Maybe you or someone you know has desired something for a long time, but then—unexpectedly—still felt empty after getting it.

We all want to avoid being unhappy, but often we don't seem to know how—or, since we live in a world with evil and suffering, if it's even possible.

It's strange that we need happiness so much and can still know so little about what it is. This series is dedicated to helping you understand more deeply what happiness is and examine how you are pursuing happiness in your own life.

**NOTES**

# Lesson One—The Four Levels of Happiness

Episode Timecode
**2:39**

## The Importance of Happiness

Even when we may not know how to find happiness, we know we need it.

Humankind has always been preoccupied with the search for happiness. From the beginning of history, virtually every philosopher from Plato and Aristotle to modern scientists such as Albert Einstein have held up happiness as one of the most important things that we can reflect on in life.

Why? Because everything else in our life depends on it. As Aristotle explains, "Happiness is the one thing you can choose for itself; everything else is chosen for the sake of happiness."

 **Plato**
(428–347 B.C.)

*Greek philosopher*

One of the earliest, most influential thinkers of Western Civilization, he founded one of its first schools, the Academy. His best-known works are his *Dialogues* and the *Republic*.

 **Aristotle**
(384–322 B.C.)

*Greek philosopher*

A student of Plato, his many writings laid the foundation for subjects as varied as biology and theater, aesthetics and physics, ethics and linguistics. His study of happiness is found in the *Nichomachean Ethics*.

## NOTES

**Albert Einstein**
(1879–1955)

*Groundbreaking 20th-century theorist and scientist*

His investigations into the nature of the universe produced such landmarks as the theory of relativity and the theory of matter-energy equivalence (source of the famous equation $E=mc^2$).

 **PHILOSOPHY (FROM GREEK, "LOVE OF WISDOM"):**

The study of the most fundamental realities, such as the meaning of existence and the nature of consciousness, by systematic thought.

 **PSYCHOLOGY (FROM GREEK, "STUDY OF THE SOUL"):**

The science of the mind; investigating how the mind works and how to foster mental health.

 **ANTHROPOLOGY (FROM GREEK, "STUDY OF MAN"):**

The study of human beings through science, history, and culture.

 **THEOLOGY (FROM GREEK, "STUDY OF GOD"):**

The study of God and by extension the study of religious truths and supernatural realities (e.g., angels, Purgatory, the Incarnation).

**NOTES**

"Happiness is the **one** thing you can choose for itself; **everything else** is chosen for the sake of happiness."

— **Aristotle,** *Nichomachean Ethics*

# Lesson One—The Four Levels of Happiness

## Happiness and Life Goals

Since happiness is the only thing chosen for itself, that means that our happiness will be the main goal that shapes every other decision in our life.

All of our life goals are steps to that ultimate destination. From whom we marry to what we eat for breakfast, every choice in our life is aiming at that one final result—the happy version of you.

### How Happiness Influences Our Life:

- What We Strive For
- The Friendships We Make
- The Careers We Pursue
- The Person We Marry
- The Legacy We Leave

**NOTES**

# II. Series Overview: The Four Levels of Happiness

**NOTES**

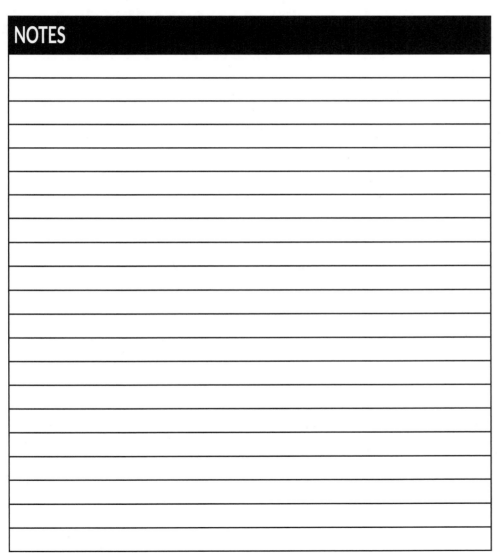

## The Four Levels of Happiness:

 1. Pleasure (*Laetus*)

 2. Success (*Felix*)

 3. Making a Difference (*Beatus*)

 4. Transcendence (*Sublimitas*)

### Level 1—Pleasure

 Episode Timecode
**5:03**

The first level is pleasure, which comes from external things. Many of these pleasures come from satisfying our physical needs such as food, clothing, or shelter, and they fade quickly once the need is met.

## Level 2—Success

 Episode Timecode
**7:02**

The second level goes beyond the external senses to an internal sense of self. How do I measure up to others?

> **EGO-CENTRIC**
>
> Believing that everything in the outside world revolves around oneself. Ego-centric people do not recognize the importance, feelings, or perspectives of others.

### Ego-Comparative:
### Inner World vs. Outer World

We are aware first of ourselves and then of the world around us.

Ego-comparative happiness is when we compare ourselves (*ego* = self) to others and judge that we are better.

### Achievement, Status, Popularity

The main ways we can rank ourselves against other people are through these:

- **Achievements:** Harvard Graduate, State Wrestling Champ, Gold Medalist, Valedictorian, Academy Award Winner, Guiness World Record for Sweater-Knitting

- **Status:** Vice-President of a Fortune 500 Company, Head Cheerleader, Town Council, U.N. Council, Seat at the Cool Kids Table

- **Popularity:** Most Friends, Most Online "Friends", Starring Role in the Play

**NOTES**

# The Comparison Game

## Winner ...

## ... or Loser?

## Winners and Losers

Comparisons with others means that for you to be a "winner" you need to be better than other people—who thus have to be "losers".

Many people who focus on comparisons will find themselves uncomfortably in the middle, better than some people but not as good as others.

Are they winners or losers, then?

### NOTES

# Lesson One—The Four Levels of Happiness

## The Need for More—Competition and Unhappiness

With so many people in the world, a need to exceed others can never be completed: you will always need to be more, and what you have will never be enough.

You can't enjoy being the best, since it's always threatened by fear that someone better could turn up. This is how many apparently successful people can be so unhappy and even self-destructive.

**NOTES**

---
---
---
---
---
---
---
---
---
---
---
---
---
---
---
---
---
---

## "The person who dies with the most toys, wins."

**— Popular expression of Level 2 focus**

## Level 3—
## Making a Difference

Episode Timecode
**9:44**

The third level is based on our desire to contribute something to the world around us, for our lives to make a difference.

### Desire for Significance

We want our lives to matter. Sometimes we feel this need the opposite way: we don't want our lives to be meaningless or insignificant.

We want to feel the world is better off because we were in it, and not that we made it worse.

---

## The Sources of Contributive Happiness

- Doing
- "Being With"

---

### Contributive Happiness

The desire for significance can be satisfied by doing things that contribute something to the world, and also by simply being with others in a meaningful and unselfish way.

**CONTRIBUTIVE DRIVE**
The natural drive each person has to make a difference in the world, to contribute to the well-being of others.

**NOTES**

# Lesson One—The Four Levels of Happiness

"The true meaning of life is to be discovered **in the world** rather than **within man** or his own [mind], as though it were a closed system …

The **more one forgets himself—** by giving himself to a *cause to serve* or another *person to love*—the **more human he is**."

—**Victor Frankl,** *Man's Search for Meaning*

### Not a Competition

Bringing more goodness into the world is satisfying in itself, rather than for the success it brings.

Yet, people can sometimes turn this into a Comparison Game: "I did more good than you did, therefore my life is better than yours", which reintroduces Level 2 and all its insecurity.

**NOTES**

## Giving Your Best vs. Being Better

So how can Level 3 be different? Instead of asking, "Am I better than others?", the contributive drive in Level 3 makes us ask, "Did I use whatever I had to do as much good as I could?"

The happiness that comes from doing as much good with our lives as we can isn't threatened by whether others can do more or less.

**Viktor Frankl**
**(1905–1997)**

*Psychiatrist and philosopher*

Best known for his 1946 book, *Man's Search for Meaning*, detailing his own experience in the Nazi concentration camps and the search for purpose in existence even under the darkest conditions.

# Contributive Happiness

**vs.**

- Doing
- Being With

- Disengaged
- Loneliness

## NOTES

## Level 4—Transcendence: Our Purpose Beyond the World

Episode Timecode
**13:53**

Level 3 moves us to bring goodness into the world. Level 4 stirs us with the sense that we are destined for a goodness that goes beyond this world, that transcends it.

### The Heart's Desire Beyond the World.

The stirring of the heart that we are destined for something more is found in art and literature throughout history.

An early famous instance is Saint Augustine's *Confessions*, written 1,600 years ago, which described his own journey toward happiness and stated that we have certain desires for perfect things that can't be satisfied by the imperfect things in our world.

### The Five Transcendent Desires

From our earliest childhood, we have an instinctive desire for perfect truth, perfect love, perfect goodness or justice, perfect beauty, and perfect home.

When we see a beautiful face or flower fading with time, when we lose a friend or have to leave a home that has made us feel loved and secure—these imperfect experiences leave us with a desire for a perfect, unfailing kind of experience.

**TRANSCENDENT DESIRES**

Desires that seek perfection in truth, love, goodness, beauty, and home. These desires reveal our awareness of perfection *beyond* anything that can be learned from this world—and so they are called "transcendent"—a word that goes "beyond".

**NOTES**

**NOTES**

### The Quest for the Perfect

The realization that everything in the world is imperfect, including ourselves, means that our quest for perfection must lead us somewhere outside of ourselves and even beyond the world.

This is what led Saint Augustine to pursue God, saying, "For Thou hast made us for Thyself, and our hearts are restless until they rest in Thee."

**Saint Augustine**
(354–430)

*Catholic bishop whose influential writings on theology earned him the title "Doctor of the Church"*

He narrates his own conversion from a life of sin and pleasure to a life devoted to God in his *Confessions* (written in 398).

## The Five Transcendent Desires

- Truth
- Love
- Goodness/Justice
- Beauty
- Home

# Lesson One—The Four Levels of Happiness

## Invitation from God

Saint Augustine's quotation illustrates that this desire for perfection comes from an awareness in our hearts that there is something greater out there, and the awareness moves us to seek it out.

He believed that this awareness itself comes from God, who is inviting us to find our transcendent purpose.

**TRINITY**

The Christian teaching that there is only One God in Three Persons (Father, Son, and Holy Spirit). Most Christian faiths share this belief and regard it as a profound mystery.

**SACRAMENTS (FROM LATIN, "MADE HOLY")**

In the Catholic Church, the sacraments are visible rituals that are channels through which God confers his presence and his grace to people.

> "For Thou hast made us for Thyself, and our hearts are **restless** until they **rest in Thee**."
>
> —**Saint Augustine**, *The Confessions*

**NOTES**

**FOUR LEVELS OF DESIRE-HAPPINESS**

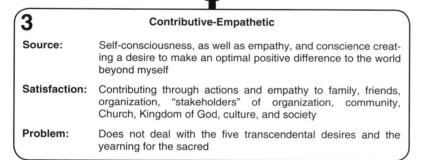

**4**     **Transcendent**

Source:    Transcendental awareness of and desire for the sacred and spiritual as well as perfect and unconditional truth, love, justice-goodness, beauty, and being (home)

Satisfaction:    Openness to a transcendental power who is perfect and unconditional truth, love, justice or goodness, beauty, and being (home)

Problem:    Not maintaining life of prayer and moral-spiritual connection

**3**     **Contributive-Empathetic**

Source:    Self-consciousness, as well as empathy, and conscience creating a desire to make an optimal positive difference to the world beyond myself

Satisfaction:    Contributing through actions and empathy to family, friends, organization, "stakeholders" of organization, community, Church, Kingdom of God, culture, and society

Problem:    Does not deal with the five transcendental desires and the yearning for the sacred

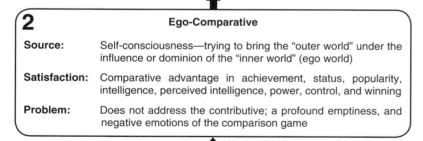

**2**     **Ego-Comparative**

Source:    Self-consciousness—trying to bring the "outer world" under the influence or dominion of the "inner world" (ego world)

Satisfaction:    Comparative advantage in achievement, status, popularity, intelligence, perceived intelligence, power, control, and winning

Problem:    Does not address the contributive; a profound emptiness, and negative emotions of the comparison game

**1**     **External-Pleasure-Material**

Source:    Brain and sensory faculties

Satisfaction:    Food, drink, shelter, affection, procreation, and material satisfaction—clothes, house, car, jewelry, and other material goods

Problem:    Superficial, profound emptiness, reduces self to the merely material

# III. Conclusion: Our Experience of Happiness

## Do You Recognize the Four Levels of Happiness?

Episode Timecode
**22:11**

When you think of your own idea of happiness, does it match up with something from one or more of the four levels?

Are the desires of each level familiar to you?

## How Have You Experienced Happiness in Your Own Life?

Our English language uses one word for all of them, but understanding the distinctions between the four levels can transform how we look at our own experiences of happiness.

In future lessons we will explore how the different levels work together: sometimes we can encounter different levels of happiness in the same experience, and in other experiences we can find different levels giving us competing impulses.

**NOTES**

# Lesson One—The Four Levels of Happiness

 **SMALL GROUP REFLECTION & DISCUSSION QUESTIONS**

1. Why are some people unhappy and happy at the same time—full and empty, fulfilled and unfulfilled?

2. Why do some teenagers who have great potential have suicidal feelings?

3. Why do some extremely gifted people resent so deeply the little successes of people who do not have nearly as much—and even belittle those successes?

4. Why do we sometimes move from a sense of superiority and contempt to a sense of inferiority and fear over the course of just a few minutes?

5. Why do some people who have every imaginable form of giftedness and success drink or drug themselves into oblivion and failure?

6. What does happiness mean to you?

7. What is a life goal that you have chosen based on your idea of happiness?

8. What is a choice you often face that forces you to pick between two different levels of happiness?

9. Can you recall a specific moment in your life where you felt a transcendent desire, something more than the world could offer?

**NOTES**

# Lesson Two—The Comparison Game

## I. Which Level of Happiness Is Dominant?

The four levels of happiness are interconnected, and there is a natural progression moving up the four levels. However, one of the four levels is going to be most dominant in a person's life.

### Review of the Four Levels

**Level 1:**

*Getting pleasure from something else*

**Level 2:**

*Ego-boosting*

**Level 3:**

*Making a contribution and leaving a legacy*

**Level 4:**

*Finding ultimate purpose and eternal destiny, leading us to the feeling of "home"*

 **EGO**

The self (from the Latin for "I"). It can also refer to an inflated sense of self or focus on self; hence, a proud person has a big "ego".

Episode Timecode
**1:33**

## Conflicts of Desire

One of these four levels is bound to be dominant in a person's life because of conflicts of desire—situations where one choice will enhance one level of happiness but the opposite choice will enhance a different level of happiness. Which choice you make reveals which level of happiness is the priority.

For instance, there is a Level 1 (pleasure) desire to eat a candy bar, but there is a Level 2 (ego/status) desire not to eat the candy bar, to avoid being overweight. Whether you choose to eat it or not eat it depends on which level is more important to you.

### NOTES

## Defining Yourself

As you repeatedly resolve conflicts of desire in favor of one particular level, that kind of happiness becomes your meaning in life. You start living for it, and the other levels fade into the background.

### NOTES

# Lesson Two—The Comparison Game

# II. The Comparison Game

**Episode Timecode**
**2:36**

Many people in our culture stay at Level 2 as their dominant level. Their happiness becomes dependent on their sense of status—how they measure up compared to everyone else.

People who get caught up in the "Comparison Game" can find themselves trapped, and moving on to Levels 3 and 4 ultimately becomes necessary if they are to avoid unhappiness. Why does this happen?

## The Benefits of Level 2

Ego-comparative happiness is worthwhile and not a bad thing in itself.

The desires of Level 2 motivate us to pursue many good things. It is very good to achieve a lot with our lives—to further our education, to have status, to have security in ourselves, to have self-esteem, to have the power to get things done.

 **EGO GRATIFICATIONS**

Anything that appeals to our sense of achievement or personal worth. These experiences are part of Level 2 happiness.

**NOTES**

Happiness | Page 26

## NOTES

 **Aaron Kheriaty**
(Living)

*Medical doctor and psychiatrist*

He has written extensively on unhappiness and depression. His study includes the negative emotional and mental health effects of the Comparison Game. He is currently Associate Professor of Psychiatry and Director of the Program in Medical Ethics at the University of California Irvine School of Medicine.

 Episode Timecode
**3:36**

## The Dangers of Level 2 Dominance

These good things are meant to lead us to deeper fulfillment. The danger comes when Level 2 becomes dominant, and achievement and status become the only things we value, the only things that make us happy. Since Level 2 should be incorporated into the higher levels, stopping there can be destructive.

### Three Groups in the Comparison Game

- The Winners
- The Losers
- The In-Between

Why is this? If your happiness depends on how highly you compare with others, there are only three possible outcomes—you succeed in being the best (winner), you fail (loser), or you fall in the middle, better than some but not as good as others. Each leads to problems.

## NOTES

## Losers

When you stake your whole sense of happiness on being the best, it obviously results in negative emotions if you lose. Feelings of inferiority, jealousy, depression, and even a sense of giving up are all common results.

### Effects of Being a Loser

- Feeling inferior
- Low self-esteem
- Jealousy
- Depression
- Lack of drive/"Giving up"

## Winners

Winning, if you are staking your whole sense of happiness on it, leads to problems as well.

## Pressures

Once you make it to the top, you face the pressure of maintaining that status. Constant vigilance is required so as not to be outdone. Lose your place at the top, and you lose your happiness—a very stressful scenario to deal with day after day.

Additionally, there is the pressure to increase your success—to recapture that feeling of accomplishment or superiority through higher and higher levels of achievement, status, intelligence, and so on.

Episode Timecode
**9:42**

## Narcisissism

"It's lonely at the top". A life devoted to being better than everyone else can frequently lead to narcissism. Nobody can stand to be around you, and (after all the effort you put into being superior to them) you can't really stand to be around them either. Narcissism thus is very lonely and can also lead to destructive treatment of others.

**NARCISSISM**

The self-centered pursuit of satisfaction through appreciation of one's own qualities, by oneself or by others.

If this wasn't enough, the isolation becomes its own problem because narcissists need the adulation of others to feed their feelings of superiority—this adulation becomes harder to get the more the narcissist drives others away, causing a cycle of frustration and anger.

Believe it or not, winners are often unhappy.

**ADULATION**

Strong and demonstrative praise.

**VICTIMIZATION**

An experience of injury or of suffering an injustice.

## Effects of Being a Winner

- Pressure to stay on top
- Insecurity that others might surpass you
- Pressure to keep accomplishing more
- Narcissism
- Isolation
- Judging others
- Alienating others

## NOTES

# Lesson Two—The Comparison Game

## In-Between

Realistically, this is the largest group, because we all have good qualities and are all imperfect—nobody can be at their best (or even at their worst) all of the time. Plus, with so many people and so many achievements to pursue, no one can be best at everything or forever. (Even an Olympic gold medalist can feel insecure about, say, a bad singing voice.)

People in-between have moments of inferiority, followed by moments of superiority, followed by moments of inferiority. They share the problems of both groups—one minute they feel the pressure and narcissism of the winner, the next they feel the jealousy and victimization of the loser. They're always questioning themselves and afraid others will start questioning them too.

## There Are No Real Winners

Each of these groups is trapped—by depression, by pressure, by self-doubt. No one wins the Comparison Game. The only way to find happiness is to escape.

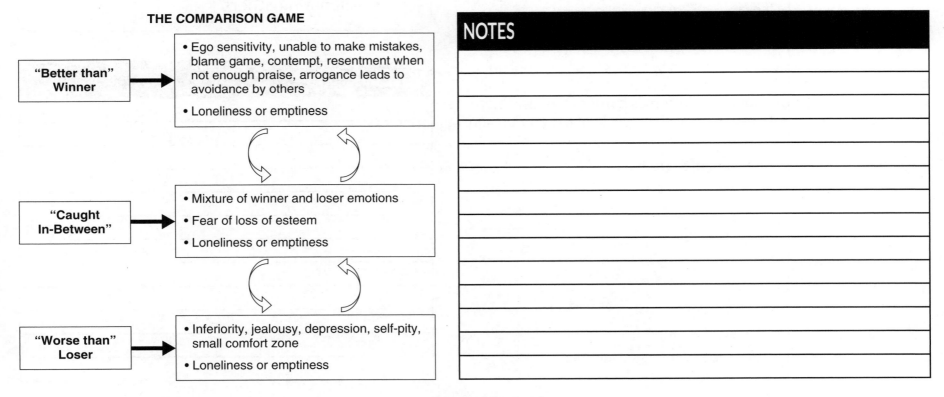

THE COMPARISON GAME

"Better than" Winner
- Ego sensitivity, unable to make mistakes, blame game, contempt, resentment when not enough praise, arrogance leads to avoidance by others
- Loneliness or emptiness

"Caught In-Between"
- Mixture of winner and loser emotions
- Fear of loss of esteem
- Loneliness or emptiness

"Worse than" Loser
- Inferiority, jealousy, depression, self-pity, small comfort zone
- Loneliness or emptiness

NOTES

## Case Study: Leah Darrow

Episode Timecode
**10:15**

Leah was drawn to the world of modeling because the models in the pictures she saw looked happy, and she wanted to be the best model so she could achieve that happiness.

Becoming a "winner" as a model required a life focused entirely on the self—self-promoting, competing for jobs, comparing her appearance with other models. The actual experience of being photographed proved to be full of pressure and anxiety about whether she was good enough and beautiful enough. It was not the happy experience she had seen in the photos.

She found happiness only after choosing to walk away from that lifestyle, shifting her focus away from the self and its status. Actively asking herself how she could be of service to others helped her break out of the Comparison Game and move onward to Level 3 and beyond.

**Leah Darrow**
(Living)

*Catholic speaker, former model*

She launched her career as a model after appearing on the reality show "America's Next Top Model". She then left the fashion world and became an advocate for Catholic causes after a moment of conversion during a photo shoot.

### CRUX

The central, most significant point. It comes from the Latin for "cross", referring to the point where two lines meet.

### COMPARISON GAME

The competition people enter into when they stake their self-worth on gaining the highest achievement, status, or popularity in comparison to other people. Level 2 is the dominant level of happiness for such people.

## NOTES

# III. Escaping the Comparison Game

 Episode Timecode **17:12** Once you decide Level 2 can't be your dominant level, where do you go? You can't simply stop pursuing status or popularity, but you have to replace it with a new goal.

## Falling Back to Level 1

Some people get out of the Comparison Game by falling back on the pleasures of Level 1. They focus their life on alcohol, drugs, adventure, expensive living, and similar experiences to escape the pain they feel from the Comparison Game.

This focus becomes self-destructive fast—if they don't get into a 12-step program or find another way to move forward into Level 3 or Level 4, they can soon find themselves on the fringes of society or even dead.

 **TWELVE-STEP PROGRAM**

A program with a set sequence of actions to follow in order to reform behavioral problems, most commonly applied to addictions such as alcoholism or drug abuse. Originally developed for Alcoholics Anonymous.

**NOTES**

# Moving Forward to Level 3

 Episode Timecode
**19:27**

## Contribution, Not Competition

A life based on competition is necessarily going to leave most people unhappy (only one person can be the best). The key to moving out of the Comparison Game is to consciously shift your focus from competition to contribution—what can I give to the people around me to make the world better?

## Life of Contribution—Family, Friends, Community

First, think about the specific contribution you want to make.

Start with the people closest to you—perhaps that friend or family member who most needs your help.

Then work your way out into the broader community. Maybe volunteer to tutor a struggling kid, or help at a community center or retirement home. What can you do for your school, or your church (for people of faith)? Is there a political or social cause you want to support?

## Positive Effects

Focusing on contributing means the emotions of the Comparison Game soon start to subside.

If you are doing the good that you can, you don't need to compare yourself to others.

You may have less talent than someone else, but if you are using more of it for good, you are objectively better off, and you know it.

---

**LIFE OF CONTRIBUTION**

A life that is habitually focused outward, naturally asking, "What can I do with what I have to improve the world and those around me?"

This focus directly contrasts with a life spent in the Comparison Game, which looks at others only to measure how they compare to the self.

# Lesson Two—The Comparison Game

## Empathy, Not Narcisissm

Episode Timecode
**20:06**

Level 2 dominance puts the focus on yourself, and this narcissism hinders your ability to have empathy for others. This makes it hard to have compassion and to want to make sacrifices for others.

How do you get out of this self-centered position?

According to philosopher Gabriel Marcel, the answer lies in changing the way we look at others. His advice is to "always look for the good news in the other."

## Looking for the Bad News

You can't look for the bad news and the good news in someone at the same time.

If you look for the bad news, you're only going to see the person as a problem, and it becomes impossible to feel empathy or compassion. You can't love the person, because you can't see them as lovable. You wind up marginalizing the person and dismissing them, closing yourself off from seeing or experiencing the good in them.

## Looking for the Good News

Luckily, the opposite also works. Look for the good news in someone, and you understand the context for the bad news (which everyone inevitably has some of). This shift in perspective makes empathy much easier.

Plus, you invariably find the little good things you would have missed: their delightful idiosyncrasies, aspirations to do good, gratuitous acts of kindness, and so on.

> ## "Always look for the good news in the other."
> ### —Gabriel Marcel

 **Gabriel Marcel**
(1879–1955)

*Philosopher and playwright*

He wrote several books that pioneered the philosophy of Personalism or "Christian Existentialism".

**NOTES**

## Positive Effects

When this new perspective leads to empathy, you get out of yourself. If you look for the good news repeatedly, it becomes a habit and starts to take you out of the narcissism, the depression, and the self-absorption of the Comparison Game.

**EMPATHY**

The ability to understand how someone is feeling, to see things from their perspective, and thus to appreciate and have care for their condition.

**IDIOSYNCRASY**

An unusual mannerism or behavior that is peculiar to one person.

## Examples of Level 3 Contributions

- Spending more time with my friends
- Spending more time with my children
- Finding ways to help people who are struggling
- Helping out at a community center
- Volunteering in the community
- Volunteering in my church
- Championing a political cause

## NOTES

# IV. The Four Levels Are a Progression

 Episode Timecode **22:01** We speak of the "four levels of happiness", not "four kinds of happiness", because they are a progression. We are naturally supposed to build from one level to the next.

## NOTES

This is why the Comparison Game and a life of pleasure cause trouble—not because they are embracing Level 1 or Level 2 happiness, but because they interrupt the natural growth that should develop and instead freeze us at these lower levels.

We can see the progression of the four levels in several ways.

### Broader Effects

Pleasures of Level 1 tend to be limited in effect to ourselves. The effects of Level 2 and Level 3 are more pervasive, reaching others in society. Indeed, Level 3 is specifically focused on reaching out to the community. The effects of Level 4, as we will see, extend the farthest—beyond this world, in fact.

### More Enduring

In addition to being broader, the effects extend further in time as you move up the levels. Level 1 pleasures don't last once they are experienced. (Eat a fine meal, and a few hours later you're hungry again.) The effects of Level 2, such as getting an education, or Level 3, such as helping others in need, can last through your whole life. The transcendent effects of Level 4 extend into eternity.

### "Deeper"

The higher levels of happiness engage a person on a "deeper" level—your highest intellectual, creative, and psychological powers. Your intelligence, your ability to love, and your awareness of the spiritual and of the infinite all come into play more as you move from pleasure to competition to contribution to transcendence.

## Approaching the Transcendentals

Finally, our focus expands toward the transcendent as we move up the levels.

Pleasures can give us a momentary encounter with goodness or beauty, for instance.

The striving for achievement in Level 2 helps us develop what is good for us, but the focus is limited to ourselves.

Level 3 expands these encounters so that we are seeking truth, love, goodness, beauty, and home for other people, but not necessarily with a focus on what is universal, ultimate, and eternal.

That focus happens in Level 4.

 **TRANSCENDENTALS**

The universal and profound goods that transcendental desires are directed to. The group, first identified in Classical philosophy, can be summarized as: Truth, Love, Goodness/Justice, Beauty, and Home.

## NOTES

# V. Conclusion

## Humans vs. Animals

Our constant striving for the transcendentals—truth, love, goodness, beauty, and home—radically separates us from all the other animal species.

Animals are content with what they are given. They are only active when their senses are awakened by an opportunity to fulfill an instinctual need—food, shelter, reproduction, or herd activity. When an animal's basic needs are met, they fall asleep.

### Animal Needs

- Food
- Shelter
- Reproduction
- Herd Activity

When a human's basic needs are met, they spend their time thinking, imagining, creating, and striving for more.

This is why the levels of happiness become progressively more pervasive, enduring, and deep—none of us really want to be superficial, to live for immediate gratification, to be reduced to the level of an animal. We want to make the most of our thoughts and actions, the most of our lives.

## Getting Stuck at a Lower Level

### Demanding Too Much

When we get stuck at Level 1 or Level 2 and make them dominant, we are demanding those deeper needs be satisfied by things that just aren't up to the task. Pleasure and success are good things, but they lead us to greater things; they can't satisfy on their own.

### Negative Effects

When the lower levels fail to satisfy, people can become self-destructive if they fail to move on to higher levels and instead seek satisfaction by doubling down and indulging more in the lower levels. People become obsessed with success or develop addictions to get more pleasure—the more dissatisfaction they feel, the more furiously they chase the obsessions and addictions, and it often becomes dangerous. This is why Thoreau said, "[Most] men lead lives of quiet desperation."

## Reaching Beyond the Lower Levels

The only alternative to this trap is to move on to the higher levels. You can begin the journey to a more meaningful life by first building these disciplines:

1. **Making a Positive Difference**

2. **Looking for the Good News in Others**

"[Most] men lead lives of quiet desperation."

—Henry David Thoreau, *Walden*

 **Henry David Thoreau**
(1817–1862)

*Philosopher and author*

He is best known for his influential book, *Walden*, reflecting on his years spent in a cabin on Walden Pond to gain perspective on nature and on modern civilization.

**NOTES**

# Lesson Two—The Comparison Game

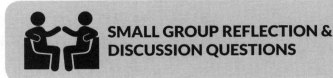

## SMALL GROUP REFLECTION & DISCUSSION QUESTIONS

1. What is a time when you experienced the negative effects associated with being a loser?

2. What is a time when you experienced the negative effects associated with being a winner?

3. When has the motivation to strive and compete led to something positive in your life?

4. Can you think of famous people who suffered from the pressures of the Comparison Game?

5. What was something you greatly looked forward to that felt different when you got it? How did you react?

6. What was something you greatly looked forward to that felt just like you expected?

7. Why wasn't Leah Darrow happy when she achieved success as a model? What did she feel she was missing? Why do you think she expected her career would make her happy?

8. What happens if you stop playing the Comparison Game without replacing it with a higher pursuit?

9. What Level 3 contribution could you easily add to your life right now? What Level 3 contribution would you find challenging?

10. Why can't you look at the bad news in someone and just force yourself to love them anyway?

**NOTES**

# Lesson Three—The Faith to Reach Transcendence

## Outline Summary

## I. The Benefits of Level 3

Even though it may seem easy to get stuck in the pursuit of pleasure or status, every person has deeper needs that call them to higher levels of happiness. It can be difficult to overcome habits that focus on the lower levels, but the effort brings us closer to our true self and gives us a liberating and renewed sense of our real purpose.

### NOTES

# Lesson Three—The Faith to Reach Transcendence

## Escaping the Comparison Game

We have seen how focusing on Level 2 happiness in the Comparison Game leaves people feeling trapped, fearful, and dissatisfied. Changing our focus from comparison to contribution frees us from the endless competition and insecure self-worth, and gives us the satisfaction of a more open life directed toward others.

## Living a Life of Contribution

Choosing a life of contribution can lead to radical changes in our life, but we can start on the path by simply asking two questions as a routine practice:

- **How can I make an optimum positive difference to my family, friends, community, and even the Kingdom of God?**

- **Am I focusing on the good news I see in others instead of the bad news?**

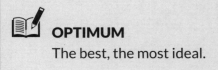

**OPTIMUM**
The best, the most ideal.

| NOTES |
| --- |

Episode Timecode
**1:33**

# II. Level 4—Happiness Is Forever

## Permanent Happiness—What Happens After Death?

Breaking out of the self-imposed hell of narcissism and developing a life of contribution can give us a renewed sense of purpose. It also raises its own question: Is making a difference and focusing on the good news in others as far as we can go?

We can go much further. All our contribution, the good we do for others, must have a purpose that aims at ultimate and lasting good. Remember our yearning for the transcendentals—we carry deep inside ourselves ideals of perfect love, perfect justice, a true home, and so on, against which we measure all our life experiences of love, justice, and home.

We can create lives that have ultimate significance and deep happiness that lasts for eternity. As we reach this ultimate level of happiness, we come across challenging questions that might not often be raised or examined in our day-to-day lives. We've reached the point in the series where we need to talk about God, particularly a loving God.

## NOTES

# Lesson Three—The Faith to Reach Transcendence

## The Importance of Evidence

Obviously, this is a weighty topic of ultimate importance, so it's important to examine the evidence for God and eternal life. The next lessons will explore a wide range of evidence, including near-death experiences, the historical examination of Jesus' Resurrection, and scientific evidence.

## The Importance of Personal Experience

It's also important to understand why the answers to these questions are personally significant, so that faith can make a transforming difference to your happiness, meaning in life, and eternal future. Hence, we begin by looking at the notable effects of faith that contribute to happiness, learned by observing these effects in actual people of faith today.

**HUMILITY**

An awareness of our true state. Humility is an important aid in opening ourselves up to the contributive and transcendent levels of happiness. It is important not to confuse humility (as often happens) with low self-esteem or the habit of belittling oneself, traits that have more in common with the Comparison Game.

**GRATITUDE**

A feeling of appreciation for benefits we have received. Cultivated as a habit, gratitude is a virtue that orients us toward generosity and engagement with the world around us and away from anxiety and selfishness.

**NOTES**

Episode Timecode
**2:50**

## Case Study: Eduardo Verástegui

Born in a small town in Mexico, Eduardo Verástegui had a meteoric rise to fame, touring internationally in a boy band by age 19. Upon moving to the United States, he won a leading film role with a major studio in his very first English-language audition, and was simultaneously hired by Jennifer Lopez to appear in her music video.

It felt as if he was living the American Dream, and he was confused to discover that, in the midst of his success, he still felt empty.

A couple providential encounters, first with an English teacher and later with a priest, opened him up to the role of faith. His teacher confronted him with deeper questions, such as these:

- What is the purpose of life?
- How are you using your talents?
- Who is God in your life?
- Are you part of the problem or part of the solution?

Eduardo realized that in his media appearances he was not serving as a good role model; previously he had not even considered his responsibilities, because of his Level 2 focus on his success and fame. He made the move from the Comparison Game to a life of contribution, making a promise not to do anything as a performer to offend his faith, his family, or his Latino culture.

This promise meant a great career sacrifice—none of the roles offered him in the next *four years* met this new standard, and he turned them all down.

He was facing the end of his career, but he was okay with it. He had lost everything, but had found everything that matters. Replacing his career, his faith now slowly became the center of his life.

He had a new purpose in his life—to give himself completely to God, who had created him with a mission. The anxiety and fear he used to live with were replaced with peace and trust in God.

> "From now on, I **only want** to be in projects that will make the world a **better place.**"
>
> —Eduardo Verástegui

# Lesson Three—The Faith to Reach Transcendence

## NOTES

## The Role of Faith

Episode Timecode
**13:12**

### Humility—I Know Who I Am and I'm Not Worried

A clear-eyed and secure sense of who we are is a great antidote to the self-obsession and inflated sense of self in the Comparison Game. Arrogance turns the focus inward, but often the only apparent alternative is "phony humility", where we downplay ourselves, even though we don't really believe that's accurate. But if we're not all-important, and we're not worthless, what are we?

How do we gain a clear sense of who we are? How do we escape from the constant anxiety and insecurity of the Comparison Game? Faith in God can give people this openness because it gives them a concrete perspective on a world greater than themselves.

**NOTES**

## Gratitude—Looking for the "Good News" in Our Whole Lives

Gratitude for what we have been given frees us to see the positive side of life. Grateful people try to help others, and this open, outward-looking disposition means they naturally adopt the life of contribution.

Ingratitude, by contrast, makes us closed off, grasping at what we have and being jealous of others. This disposition makes it harder to enjoy what we have and closes us off from the higher levels of happiness.

# Lesson Three—The Faith to Reach Transcendence

## "Mystical" Vision of the World—Seeing the Loving Creator through the World around Us

Many people come to a belief in God through philosophy or science, finding signs of a Creator in the physical universe. Faith takes this further, seeing not only the intelligence of a Supreme Being in math and science, but also the love of that Supreme Being in the world and how it corresponds to what Jesus tells us about the unconditional love of God.

## NOTES

 Episode Timecode
**14:38**

### Case Study: Dr. John Lennox

Dr. John Lennox is a Professor of Mathematics at Oxford University, and a person of faith with intense intellectual curiosity.

From his childhood on, he always experienced faith as something open to the big questions and open to being questioned. As a professor, this developed into a decision to befriend people who didn't share his worldview in order to find out what their questions were. Interested in the interface of science, philosophy, and theology to address the big questions of existence and eternity, Dr. Lennox has found that the more he has exposed his faith in God to questioning and weighed the evidence, the stronger his faith has grown.

### The Gift of Guidance—Free to Let God Bring Our Life Where It's Meant to Be

Faith brings us to the loving God and frees us to put ourselves in his hands—and to let Him, who sees what no human being can see, bring us to a much fuller meaning and significance in both this life and the next.

## Connecting to Our Creator: A Relationship with God

Episode Timecode
**25:45**

Faith in God gives these gifts because people of faith know their place in the world and what they were called to do and be. As we consider Level 4 happiness, we can see this ultimate calling:

God has created us to be in a relationship with Him from the moment of our conception, which is why we have a natural propensity to seek him.

How do we approach God's presence within us? We do so through the five transcendentals and through our natural proclivity toward the sacred and transcendent.

**PROPENSITY**

A habitual tendency.

**PROCLIVITY**

Natural tendency toward or inclination.

**ATHEIST**

Someone who believes that there is no God, often accompanied by a denial of any transcendent world beyond our own visible one. Distinct from an Agnostic, who professes not to know whether or not God exists (and who, in some cases, may profess that the existence of God is unknowable ever).

**NOTES**

## Five Transcendentals

Since the time of Plato, philosophers have reflected on five desires that seem to be almost inexhaustible. We desire these things in a perfect form.

- **Truth**

  Human beings want to know everything about everything, and we know when we don't know everything about everything. In that case, where did we get a sense of everything about everything? It must have been placed in us—as Eddington says, "The light beckons ahead and the purpose surging in our nature responds."

- **Love**

  We want unconditional love, and we always know when love is not unconditional—when it is not perfect. But how can we always recognize imperfect love unless we have a sense of perfect love?

- **Goodness and Justice**

  We live in a world of much injustice, and we are not content, because it fails to measure up to the sense of perfect justice we have inside us. Since perfect justice is not to be found in this world, where does that sense originate?

**UNCONDITIONAL LOVE**

Love directed toward someone without any reservation whatsoever—it does not decline over time, in difficult circumstances, or if either person changes, and it does not need to be earned. Thus it has no conditions and is unconditional.

**NOTES**

 **Sir Arthur Eddington**
(1882–1944)

*Astronomer, physicist*

An accomplished scientist in his own right, he also wrote many popular works explaining cutting-edge science such as the Theory of Relativity for the general public. Like John Lennox today, Eddington was also interested in exploring the interface of science with philosophy and religion.

 **Saint Thomas Aquinas**
(1225–1274)

*Philosopher, theologian*

Best known for his encylopedic works of theology, *Summa Theologica* and *Summa contra Gentiles*, Aquinas was a leader in exploring the interface of faith and reason, working to integrate classic philosophy (primarily through Aristotle) with Christianity's teachings on God and religious questions.

- **Beauty**

  Think how much of the Comparison Game is fueled by the constant pursuit of perfect beauty. In the Comparison Game, this desire is always frustrated. But if perfect beauty is elusive in this world, where is it to be found? Where does that desire come from?

- **Home**

  One of the striking benefits of the gift of faith, as seen in the case studies we've looked at, is the confidence and security faith brings. These people of faith know where they are going. They have an answer to the yearning found in song and story throughout human history for a more perfect place, a land where we truly belong, a lost paradise.

## Desire Comes from God's Perfection

It seems, then, that we have five ideas of the perfect and unconditional within us that we could have never gotten from our brains and the world. The only source seems to be the very ideas themselves. That is why Plato, Augustine, Aquinas, and modern philosophers such as Maritain, Lonergan, Adler, Rahner, and many others believe that God is present to us.

 **Jacques Maritain**
(1882–1973)

*Philosopher*

Much of his work is devoted to continuing Aquinas' integration of faith and reason in the fields of modern philosophical and scientific study.

 **Mortimer Adler**
(1902–2001)

*Philosopher*

A modern student of Aristotle and Aquinas, he wrote books intended for a mass audience on issues such as freedom, human nature, and religion.

 **Bernard Lonergan**
(1904–1984 )

*Priest, philosopher*

His writings seek to integrate modern scientific thought and the principles of Christianity, similar to what Aquinas did with the natural philosophy of his time.

## NOTES

Episode Timecode
**33:19**

## Man's Primordial Invitation to the Transcendent

### The Universal "Idea of the Holy"

Almost everyone around the world is intensely religious (currently 84 percent of the human population is, and even that number is historically low). So universal is this human behavior, that philosophers have been led to study why. Rudolph Otto and Mircea Eliade are among the philosophers who have studied how religion is a part of our lives. The experience of religion throughout the world seems to share an internal and external component.

**PRIMORDIAL**

From the very beginning, fundamental.

**NOTES**

## NOTES

 **Rudolf Otto**
(1859–1937)

*Theologian, scholar*

He introduced the notion of the "numinous experience" (derived from *numen*, the Latin term for "divine power") in his popular work *The Idea of the Holy* in 1917.

 **Mircea Eliade**
(1921–1986)

*Philosopher, historian of religion*

An academic of many interests, Eliade wrote extensively on religion in society, including the significance of ritual and the presence of the sacred.

### Numinous Experience

The numinous experience refers to a person's awareness of the presence of the transcendent within us. We experience it as mysterious, overwhelming, "wholly other"; it moves us to an awareness that we are creatures. One might assume this experience would be negative, inspiring fear or a depressing inferiority, but the opposite is true.

It holds out the potential for us to be complete, even to be loved. It fascinates us and makes us want to draw toward it and this greater reality. We experience this transcendent reality as positive—in fact, as the ultimate good.

This internal draw toward the transcendent is so strong in our nature that psychologists have been led to study it. Additionally, people frequently show great inner distress when they abandon religion. Psychologists have observed that many psychological problems, including increased suicide rates, occur when people are not religiously affiliated.

## The Numinous Experience

Suppose you were told there was a tiger in the next room: you would know that you were in danger and would probably feel fear. But if you were told, "There is a ghost in the next room", and believed it, you would feel, indeed, what is often called fear, but of a different kind. It would not be based on the knowledge of danger, for no one is primarily afraid of what a ghost may do to him, but of the mere fact that it is a ghost. It is "uncanny" rather than dangerous, and the special kind of fear it excites may be called Dread. With the Uncanny one has reached the fringes of the Numinous.

Now suppose that you were told simply, "There is a mighty spirit in the room", and believed it. Your feelings would then be even less like the mere fear of danger: but the disturbance would be profound. You would feel wonder and a certain shrinking—a sense of inadequacy to cope with such a visitant, of prostration before it.... This feeling may be described as awe, and the object which excites it as the Numinous.

— C. S. Lewis, *The Problem of Pain*

 **C. S. Lewis**
**(1898–1963)**

*Writer and scholar*

Famous both for his novels and for his nonfiction books on Christianity, he wrote fiction that often deals with people encountering timeless spiritual truths in a world beyond our own, in fantasy (*The Chronicles of Narnia*) as well as in science fiction (*The Space Trilogy*).

**NOTES**

## External Expression

Episode Timecode
**38:18**

This numinous experience does not remain merely internal. People throughout the world who encounter this experience also sense that a greater reality has broken into our world and extended us an invitation. Hence, the movement to worship takes on external forms: a church, rituals, symbols, a religious community. Time and again, religious traditions invoke the image of a final banquet, a wedding feast or some sort of communal celebration. Ultimately, we share this transcendent experience as a community.

**NOTES**

# III. Conclusion—The Life of Faith

Faith leads to so many new things for our lives because it opens us up to the transcendent, which is the aim of Level 4 happiness.

Once we move outside ourselves (Level 2) to a concern for others (Level 3), we are faced with the wider world, in which we discover a loving Creator calling us to our transcendent destiny (Level 4) and a shared eternal relationship with Him.

**NUMINOUS EXPERIENCE**

The inner encounter with the transcendent and the sacred. It evokes a complex combination of fearful awe and fascination that makes the person feel called to draw toward it.

**NOTES**

# Lesson Three—The Faith to Reach Transcendence

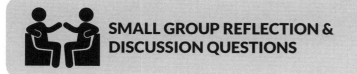

**SMALL GROUP REFLECTION & DISCUSSION QUESTIONS**

1. Is making a difference and focusing on the good news in others as far as we can go? Why or why not?

2. What is the purpose of life?

3. How are you using your talents?

4. Who is God in your life?

5. Are you part of the problem or part of the solution?

6. What could be examples of encounters with something transcendental?

7. What are the reactions evoked by the numinous experience? Is there a time when you have experienced these emotions?

**NOTES**

# Lesson 4—Level 4 Evidence: Near-Death Experiences

But is this true? We need to know if God exists and if the life after death that people feel called to is real.

When we are looking at evidence for life after death, near-death experiences can provide medical evidence pointing to the survival of human consciousness after bodily death.

## I. What Is a Near-Death Experience?

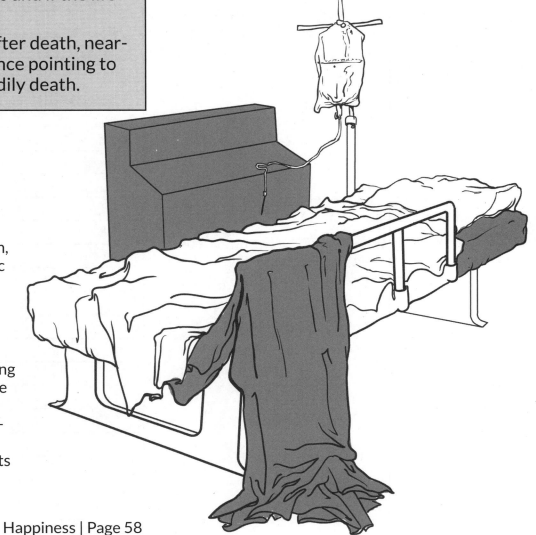

In thousands of clinically monitored cases of clinical death, the patients have reported a similar phenomenon, what we now call a near-death experience. Several basic elements recur across these reports.

### Awareness Outside Their Body

For the typical patients, the experience begins with the consciousness leaving the body—often described as going through a tunnel and coming out—and hovering over the body, so they can "see" their body as well as the activity going on around it in the hospital. They are fully aware—not only able to sense things by seeing and hearing, but able to recall past memories and to remember the events they have witnessed while unconscious (and to recount them afterward, as we will see below).

## Experiencing the Transcendent

This awareness transcends the normal sense experiences of daily life in several ways:

### 1. Free from Physical Laws

The person's consciousness in these reports is not subject to physical laws during the experience:

They can pass through walls.

They can move up in the air unrestrained by gravity.

They can move with inordinate speed.

### 2. Moving to Another World

Many report moving from this world altogether, into another world that is transcendent, beautiful, and peaceful.

### 3. Encountering Others

Those who move into this other world frequently see deceased relatives and friends. These loved ones are transformed from how they were in life:

They are youthful (even if they died old).

They seem to have a spiritual quality.

They manifest extraordinary wisdom, peace, and love.

They are recognizably themselves, however, and will greet and converse with the person.

**NEAR-DEATH EXPERIENCE**

Phenomena reported by people who have seen and experienced things while they were clinically dead (and thus incapable of sensing anything with their physical senses or brain).

**NOTES**

## Overwhelming Love

Perhaps the most well-known pattern in these reports is the white light that people encounter, a light that is incredibly bright but does not cause pain. The light is filled with overwhelming love and seems to know everything about the person. Some people, particularly children, see Jesus.

# II. Alternative Explanations

## Clinical Death

Episode Timecode
**3:07**

While the detailed similarities among the many cases are striking, it is still challenging to explain from a physical perspective how they happen in the first place, since the subjects are all clinically dead at the time.

Clinical death means a person is brain-dead—simply put, the brain has ceased to function. The main indicators of brain death are a flat EEG, fixed and dilated pupils, and the absence of gag reflex. Taken together, these indicate an absence of electrical activity in the brain and a failure to perform even involuntary functions (a clinically dead person will not breathe, and their heart will not beat, requiring life-support to continue).

Without brain function, we can be sure that the sensing and thoughts and memories of the clinically dead person are not occuring through his organic brain. What, then, are their cause?

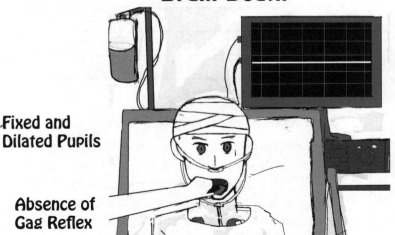

**Brain Death**

Flat EEG

Fixed and
Dilated Pupils

Absence of
Gag Reflex

**NOTES**

## Suggested Physical Causes

Some people believe a physical cause can be found—suggested explanations include hallucinations, deprivation of oxygen, narcotics, or the shutdown of the brain. All of these arguments propose some form of physically or chemically induced malfunction in the brain that produces the sights, sounds, thoughts, and memories of the experience.

 **CLINICAL DEATH**

A technical term that essentially refers to "brain death" when there is next to no electrical activity in the brain, rendering thinking processes virtually impossible. Since brain function has stopped, the use of respirators and other life-support systems are required to keep involuntary processes such as breathing and circulation going in the clinically dead patient, and without such interference, these involuntary processes stop as well.

## Alternate Theories for Near-Death Experiences

- Hallucinations

- Deprivation of Oxygen

- Narcotics (used for pain or resuscitation)

- Shutdown of the Brain

**NOTES**

# III. Evidence for a Nonphysical Cause

If these causes are excluded, this would indicate that the human person has a transphysical dimension to it, something akin to a soul. In other words, it would indicate our consciousness is distinct from our organic brains, since it is able to sense and think in the absence of physical brain activity.

Several sources of evidence do in fact seem to exclude physical explanations of near-death experiences.

## Monitoring the Brain: Dr. Janice Holden

 Episode Timecode
**4:26**

The most immediate issue with physical explanations of near-death experiences, all of which attribute them to malfunctioning brain behavior, is that there is *no* activity in the brain during the experience. We know this because the documented cases being studied occur in hospitals, and the brain is typically being monitored. The flat EEG indicating the absense of any brain activity (malfunctioning or otherwise) is one of the key factors in diagnosing clinical death in the first place.

Any cognitive functions reported by the patient, therefore, had to be performed outside of his physical body.

 **TRANSPHYSICAL SOUL**
A soul that exists independently of the physical body.

 **Dr. Janice Holden**
(Living)

*Researcher of Near-Death Experiences*
A widely published researcher in the field, she is president of the International Association for Near-Death Studies. Dr. Holden received her doctorate in education from Northern Illinois University and is Professor and Chairperson of Counseling and Higher Education at the University of North Texas.

**NOTES**

## Blind People in Near-Death Experiences: Dr. Kenneth Ring

Episode Timecode
**14:55**

A controlled scientific study of the near-death experiences of blind people revealed that the blind experienced sight during their experience just as others did. Many of these people were blind from birth, and thus had no prior experience of sight, which they reported as being initially disorienting (though often deeply moving as well) during the near-death experience.

Here, then, is a form of sensory awareness that is not only inexplicable during clinical death, but goes beyond the physical abilities of the patient's brain during normal life.

 **VERIDICAL DATA**

Data that can be verified after the fact by the observations of a third party. Such data, as a rule, is concerned with facts about the documentable physical world.

 **Dr. Kenneth Ring**
(Living)

He authored the study on near-death experiences of blind people, primarily the blind from birth. He received his doctorate from UCLA and became a professor of psychology at the University of Connecticut, where he has catalogued near-death experiences through controlled scientific studies.

## NOTES

# Lesson Four—Level 4 Evidence: Near-Death Experiences

## Veridical Data—A Study of Studies

Episode Timecode
**16:35**

Veridical data refers to data that can be verified after the fact by the observations of a third party. While many elements of a near-death experience take place in an unreachable world and cannot be verified directly by observation, the things that people witness in this world and remember afterward can be verified. Dr. Holden took thirty-seven clinically controlled studies and made a study of the veridical data in all 37 of them (which spanned hundreds of cases).

Some near-death experience details can't be observed or verified by someone else

Veridical Data:
Details that can be verified by someone else

She found that the veridical data was reported more accurately by the clinically dead than by the other people in the hospital room. In some cases, the details being reported and independently verified involved distant or inaccessible areas of the hospital, or conversations overheard while the brain was being actively monitored and failing to register activity.

Again, we see conscious activity that exceeds not only the limitations of the clinically dead but the physical abilities of the healthy.

### NOTES

# IV. Conclusion

Episode Timecode
**23:17**

## The Evidence of Near-Death Experiences

The veridical data, the vision of blind people, and the many highly monitored and controlled studies of near-death experiences make it difficult to deny the existence of a transphysical soul: a soul that survives bodily death and can see, hear, remember, think, feel—and even transcend the laws of physics.

Another important suggestion from these studies is the existence of a transphysical world: a world where the deceased live transformed. This world is overseen by a loving white light that reveals the loving nature of the afterlife.

**NOTES**

## The Personal Implications of a Soul

The existence of the soul is not simply an academic or scientific question.

How does it change your life if you know you are going to endure beyond death? How do you treat other people if every one of them is destined for a transcendent existence? How do the difficulties and even the despair you may sometimes face in life change, if there is something more that comes after this life altogether? The existence of a transcendent world, a loving destiny beyond this life, is of great personal importance. We have seen the evidence of near-death experiences—in the next lesson we will examine a different source of evidence.

# Lesson Four—Level 4 Evidence: Near-Death Experiences

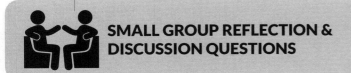

**SMALL GROUP REFLECTION & DISCUSSION QUESTIONS**

1. Why does it matter whether or not we have a consciousness that survives death?

2. What similarities do the near-death experiences described in this chapter share?

3. What physical explanations are proposed for near-death experiences during clinical death? What counterarguments are given?

4. How would you treat a "clump of molecules" differently from a "transcendent being"? How do you see yourself?

5. What aspects of near-death experiences point to a God of unconditional love?

6. What is a time in your life when you felt called to unconditional love? What is a time in your life when you felt you weren't called to anything, or felt despair? What can you learn from comparing them?

7. If God is calling you to an eternal life in unconditional love, what does that say about how you should relate to others?

8. How does having a soul affect the way you view your self-worth, and the self-worth of others?

9. How does your destiny after death (and whether you have one at all) affect the way you live your life?

**NOTES**

# Lesson Five—Level 4 Evidence: The Resurrection

## Outline Summary

We looked at near-death experiences and the evidence they show about the soul and the afterlife. These correlate with the teachings and Resurrection of Jesus. Jesus said the afterlife will be eternal and that we will be brought to a state of unconditional love. But Jesus offered a more direct support for his teaching in his own Resurrection. Naturally, much study has been done on the evidence for Jesus' Resurrection.

# I. Saint Paul and the Resurrection's Witnesses

### The List of Witnesses

The offering of evidence for Jesus' Resurrection begins with Saint Paul in his First Letter to the Corinthians, written about 20 years later around A.D. 54. He gives an extensive list of witnesses who saw Jesus after the Resurrection, beginning with Saint Peter, then the other apostles, then five hundred disciples. He mentions that most of them are still living at that point, so readers can verify the story for themselves.

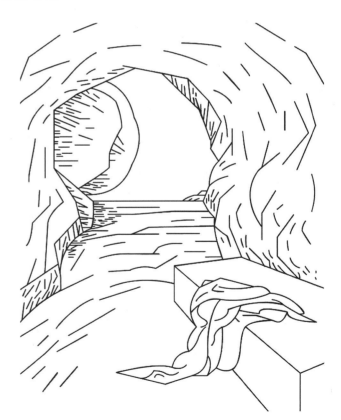

| NOTES |
|---|
|  |
|  |
|  |
|  |
|  |
|  |
|  |
|  |

## NOTES

 **Saint Paul**
(d. A.D. 67)

*Apostle*

He preached the gospel of Jesus throughout the Roman Empire, establishing or strengthing Christian communities in many cities; fourteen of the letters he wrote to these communities are included in the New Testament.

Originally a persecutor of Christians, he famously underwent a conversion on the road to Damascus when the resurrected Christ appeared to him. He himself died for the Christian faith under a Roman persecution of Christianity.

## Nothing to Gain, Everything to Lose

Saint Paul gives some context for the witnesses' stories, showing that they don't have anything to gain and a lot to lose by preaching the Resurrection.

### Religious Liars?

First, if the witnesses believe in God and are lying about the Resurrection, then they are perjuring themselves and undermining their Jewish faith for a lie for which they risk eternal punishment.

### Irreligious Liars?

Second, even if they don't believe in God, there were plenty of penalties in this world. They faced the loss of social status, financial status, and even outright persecution and death for preaching the Risen Jesus—when they supposedly knew there was no resurrection to look forward to.

## The Best Kind of Witness

Saint Paul's conclusion, of course, is that all these sacrifices the witnesses made are meaningless if they are lying. If there's no resurrection, you might as well just "eat, drink, and be merry, for tomorrow we die." Since they had nothing to gain and everything to lose by lying, it's more credible to believe they are telling the truth, since they have no incentive to make up the story.

The same techniques are used in our court systems today. Attorneys will try to prove that their witness has nothing to gain.

**NOTES**

"For I delivered to you as of first importance what I also received, that Christ died for our sins in accordance with the scriptures, that he was buried, that **he was raised on the third day** in accordance with the Scriptures,

and that **he appeared to Cephas,**

then **to the Twelve.**

Then he appeared **to more than five hundred brethren** at one time, most of whom are still alive, though some have fallen asleep."

— **Saint Paul,** *First Letter to the Corinthians 15:3–6*

# II. Modern Historical Investigation

 Episode Timecode **4:00** In modern times, historians have honed careful techniques for evaluating the historicity of events. These techniques, called "criteria for historicity", have been brought into New Testament studies by many scholars, such as Joachim Jeremias and Joseph Fitzmyer, S.J. These have brought to light some striking facts surrounding the historicity and impact of the Resurrection.

 **Joachim Jeremias**
(1900–1979)

*Scripture scholar*

He focused on the study of early Hebrew texts that would help reconstruct the historical context of Jesus' life.

 **HISTORICITY**

The existence of something in history, as distinguished from a myth, legend, or other fiction.

**NOTES**

# The Messianic Movement

## The Life Cycle of a Messiah

Due to the political turmoil in Judea at the time of Jesus, there were actually several Messianic movements. Every time one of these messiah figures was humiliated and publicly executed by the government, the movement would simply die away, no matter what steps were taken by followers to try to keep it going.

## The Growth of Christianity

Christianity, instead of disappearing, actually exploded in growth at such a rapid rate that in a few generations it would become the state religion of the empire that was trying to persecute it.

## The Difference—the Resurrection of Jesus

It's hard to imagine a more striking way Christianity could go against the pattern of Messianic movements. What was the difference? The execution of a messiah meant failure and proved they did not have the power they claimed to change history.

The narrative is different if you have witnessed your Messiah rise from the dead. Preaching the Resurrection gave a reason to continue the movement, since Jesus had proven his power over death itself and his ability to keep his promise of eternal life to humankind. Indeed, he was still keeping it through the many miracles his disciples were performing in his name.

It explains the rapid growth in the face of persecution instead of rapid death. If the Resurrection was a lie, finding the motive that explains this growth becomes much harder.

 **Saint John the Baptist**
(d. circa A.D. 31 )

*Prophet*

He preached the coming of the Messiah and repentance through Baptism. He was imprisoned by King Herod and beheaded. After his death, some of his disciples became followers of Jesus, believing him to be the promised Messiah.

## NOTES

 **Dr. Gary Habermas**
(Living)

*Scripture scholar*

He received his doctorate from Michigan State in History and the Philosophy of Religion. The author of 35 scholarly books and over 100 scholarly articles concerning the historical Jesus, he is currently a research scholar at Liberty University.

## Mutations of Second Temple Judaism

Episode Timecode
**15:10**

This is another historical aberration that seems to verify the Resurrection. Second Temple Judaism refers to the Jewish doctrines that had been formulated since the building of the Second Temple in 515 B.C. These doctrines were still current in Judaism at the time of Jesus and of the early Christians.

Historical Model of the Second Temple

## Christian Conformity

The early Christians were very respectful of the doctrines of Second Temple Judaism. They did not want to be separated from the synagogue, and so they tried to maintain continuity with this Jewish tradition as much as possible.

**NOTES**

## The Radical Exception

There are only a handful of points where the early Christians differentiated themselves strongly from the tradition, and these "mutations of Second Temple Judaism" all deal with the doctrine of the Resurrection.

In the first place, early Christians immediately placed a central emphasis on resurrection in their preaching and teaching—the whole question of resurrection was only a peripheral doctrine for Second Temple Judaism.

Moreover, Second Temple Judaism didn't even have one unified teaching on resurrection. Some believed resurrection was more of a symbolic proposition—there was life after death but not with a body. Others believed in the literal resurrection of the body. A third group, the Sadducees, didn't believe in an afterlife at all, let alone a resurrection. In contrast, early Christians from the beginning shared and preached one doctrine of actual bodily resurrection.

## The Difference—the Resurrection of Jesus

The one unified, strong disagreement from a group that was in all other respects trying to conform is much easier to explain if we take the early Christians at their word that they had witnessed Jesus after his bodily Resurrection. Their agreement and emphasis on this doctrine would be clearly motivated: the doctrinal question had just been settled for them by their Messiah's example.

 **SECOND TEMPLE JUDAISM**

The religion of Judaism as it was taught and practiced in the years between the construction of the Second Temple in 515 B.C. and its destruction in A.D. 70.

NOTES

# III. Scholarly Consensus

Episode Timecode
**22:23**

## Consensus in Survey of Scripture Scholars

A more recent case of doctrinal agreement is found in Dr. Habermas' survey of Scripture scholars. He found that the majority of Scripture scholars today agree on these two principles:

1. **Historicity of Resurrection**—The Resurrection is a real historical event, not a story invented later.
2. **Transformed Spiritual Body**—Jesus rose with a transformed body.

## Any Consensus Is Very Rare

It is unusual for these scholars, who hail from various denominations and beliefs, to reach consensus on a major doctrinal point such as this. Even those scholars who are personally agnostic or atheist acknowledge that the reports of the Resurrection can be credibly traced all the way back through history, to within a year of the event itself.

| NOTES |
| --- |
|  |
|  |
|  |
|  |
|  |
|  |

> "Eat, drink, and be merry, for tomorrow we **die**."
>
> — **Traditional saying describing the limits of life**

> "Behold, I tell you a **mystery**: We shall not all sleep, but we shall all be changed."
>
> — **Saint Paul**, *1 Corinthians 15:51*

# IV. Conclusion: Why Does It Matter?

Episode Timecode
**28:49**

## Life after Death

The historicity of Jesus' Resurrection is important on a personal level in the same way the evidence from near-death experiences was—when confirmed, it provides evidence of life after death, evidence that there is something transcendent about us beyond just our bodies, something that continues to live.

## Jesus' Role

Moreover, Jesus promised that he would rise from the dead, and that we would as well. When he rose, it showed that he could keep his promises and that he knew what he was talking about.

If Jesus was right about the existence of our eternal future, what else was he right about? He preached a God of love and a transcendent afterlife that seems to match the evidence of the near-death experiences we've seen. The next lesson will examine more closely what He had to say about the way we ought to live our lives and now the loving Father waiting for us, and how this can bring ultimate good even out of the most difficult suffering in life, which leads us ultimately to transcendent happiness.

## NOTES

# Lesson Five—Level 4 Evidence: The Resurrection

 **SMALL GROUP REFLECTION & DISCUSSION QUESTIONS**

1. What did the witnesses to the Resurrection stand to lose by lying if they believed in God? What did they stand to lose by lying even if they didn't believe in God?

2. What usually happened to a messianic movement after the messiah died? Why?

3. How was Christianity different after the death of Jesus? Why?

4. Why was it unusual for the Christians to disagree with the current Jewish doctrine? What made them do so when it came to the subject of resurrection?

5. How does the significance of near-death experiences correlate with the significance of Jesus' Resurrection?

6. Do you think the historical evidence for Jesus' Resurrection is compelling? Why or why not?

7. How is the Resurrection of Jesus relevant to the search for happiness?

## NOTES

# Lesson Six—Transcendence: Is Unconditional Love Real?

## Outline Summary

We have looked at several kinds of evidence for the existence of life after death. Both near-death experiences and the life and teaching of Jesus indicate that this afterlife will be characterized, not only by a spiritual body, but by love among all the people in the heavenly Kingdom.

For many people, though, even after the existence of God and the afterlife are established, the unconditional love of God and our destiny to share that love remains a question of its own. Is unconditional love real?

# I. Skepticism about a Loving God

There are many sources of skepticism about God's unconditional love. We live in a society of Murphy's Law, where people presume that all good news is simply too good to be true. While the existence of God and the soul are challenging enough to a habitually skeptical culture, add the concept of "love", and the skepticism intensifies.

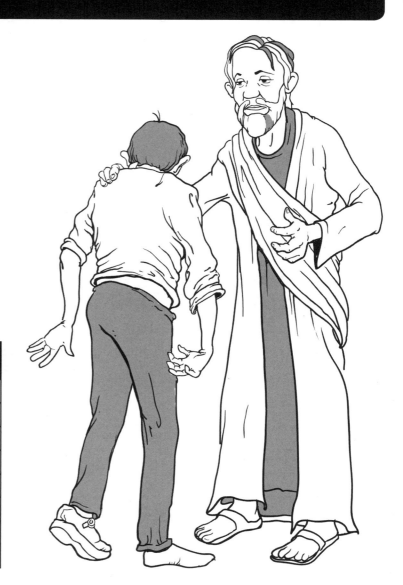

| NOTES |
|---|
|  |
|  |
|  |
|  |
|  |
|  |
|  |
|  |

# Lesson Six—Transcendence: Is Unconditional Love Real?

**MURPHY'S LAW**

An old adage to the effect of "Anything that can go wrong, will go wrong." It is often invoked in times of frustration or cynicism about life, though it also can be invoked more positively as a justification for careful and thorough planning.

**SKEPTICISM**

A questioning or doubting attitude toward accepted truths. In daily life, it can also refer to a general attitude of distrust, incredulity, or suspicion.

## God as Punishing Judge

Some people try to make Jesus into an administrator of strict justice and punishment. Many traditions and even popular culture seem to portray God's call as one focused on retribution, on exacting guilt and condemnation. The evidence from Scripture (in addition to the evidence we've reviewed) points instead to a very different reality. For Jesus, mercy trumps justice and punishment, and his love is unconditional.

## Love Is Not for Me

Others believe in a loving God, but cannot believe that they themselves are destined to receive love. Perhaps a formative experience has led them to believe that they are worthless or unlovable; or perhaps like the prodigal son they are focused on guilt for their past behavior, and seek to place conditions on God's love. Whatever the cause, they think God's love extends to everyone except them.

**NOTES**

# II. Signs of Love in Near-Death Experiences

Episode Timecode
**2:11**

As we have seen, there is much evidence to indicate that God's love is real and unconditional. Part of this evidence is found in the witness of near-death experiences.

## The Transcendent World

The existence of a transcendent world where life endures beyond death, where people are transformed into an uplifted, perfected version of their true selves, is reported time and again in these experiences.

## The Light

All the encounters with the white light consistently report it as exceedingly loving. People come away from the experience with a strong sense of love.

**NOTES**

# III. Signs of Love in Jesus

 Episode Timecode
**2:37**

We previously looked at the evidence of Jesus' Resurrection, and how it would lend credibility to his teachings. These teachings consistently emphasize God's unconditional love, as does Jesus' whole proclaimed mission of sacrificing Himself to bring humankind to salvation.

## From Intelligent Creator to Loving God

For people who recognize the scientific or philosophical evidence for the existence of a Creator, Father Spitzer draws a necessary connection between an intelligent Creator and a loving God.

The greatest power we have as creatures, the one power that can singlehandedly bring meaning and fulfillment to our lives, the one power that can never be used for evil motives, is love. If we have this power as creatures, it is difficult to hold that our Creator lacks this power. Our Creator must be loving. We know this love is unconditional through a similar line of thought—the love that we desire isn't just any love, it's perfect love. (Love is one of the transcendental desires.) Again, can we assign a lesser power to the Creator of the universe than perfect love? When we consider that the Creator who loves us gave us the desire for unconditional love, it would be inconsistent to hold that he would leave that desire unfulfilled.

By now, it makes sense that an all-powerful Creator who loves us unconditionally would want to be with us, to give himself to us, to come down to us and connect with us in a face-to-face relationship. It only remains to be asked: Is Jesus the One? Is Jesus in fact the appearance of the loving God whom we are already expecting?

**NOTES**

## NOTES

**Six Questions for "Steve": Connecting the Dots from a Creator to Jesus**

1. What's the most important power in your life, the power that can single-handedly bring happiness or purpose to your life?

2. Could the Creator of the universe lack this most meaningful power (namely, love)?

3. Do you desire just some love or perfect, unconditional love? (Have you ever been frustrated by the imperfections in someone's love? If so, what were you looking for?)

4. Do you believe the Creator who gave you that desire lacks the capacity for perfect, unconditional love?

5. Do you think a Creator would love you so unconditionally that he would want to be with you? To enter into a face-to-face relationship of perfect empathy? To become Emmanuel, "God with us"?

6. Is Jesus the One?

## The Prodigal Son

Episode Timecode
**12:41**

One of the key teachings of Jesus on God's unconditional love is found in the story he told, the Parable of the Prodigal Son. This is Jesus' consummate revelation of who God the Father is (whom he called "Abba"—affectionate and understanding "Daddy"). Notice that the father in the story is Jesus' image of God the Father. The story concerns a son who demands his share of his father's wealth and then leaves home and recklessly spends it all—betraying and shaming his family, country, religion, and God himself. In first-century Jewish terms, this son is about as bad as anyone could be. Driven to starvation, he resolves to go home, beg his father's forgiveness, and be consigned to the status of a slave.

The father—who represents God the Father—sees him coming, and instead of renouncing him for his conduct and betrayal, he rejoices and rushes to embrace him.

**PARABLE**

Story told to illustrate a teaching or moral.

**PRODIGAL**

To spend wealth excessively or wastefully; spendthrift.

**ABBA**

The Aramaic word for "Father", and the word used by Jesus in the New Testament when he preached that we should call God our Father. Most notably used in the popular prayer Jesus taught, the "Our Father".

Before the son can finish his speech, the father orders the servants to get a cloak and put it on him (indicating that he wants his son to be treated as royalty). He then asks them to bring his son sandals (to take care of his temporal needs), and then to bring the family ring. The ring is very important, because it contains the signet or sign of the family, indicating that his son belongs to the family 100 percent—no conditions, qualifications, or reservations. He then orders that the fatted calf be killed, and a celebration begins.

For Jesus, this is how God welcomes and restores every single person—even the most gravely sinful—if they but return to the Father and ask for his forgiveness.

And the son said to him, " 'Father, I have sinned against heaven and before you; I am no longer worthy to be called your son.'

But the father said to his servants, 'Bring quickly the best robe, and put it on him; and put a ring on his hand, and shoes on his feet; and bring the fatted calf and kill it, and let us eat and make merry; for this my son was dead, and is alive again; he was lost, and is found.'

And they began to make merry."

**— From the Parable of the Prodigal Son, Gospel of Luke 15:21–24**

## NOTES

# IV. Competing Views of God: The Problem of Hell

Episode Timecode
**25:38**

> Jesus' portrayal of God as a Father with unconditional love for us can seem hard to reconcile with his talk of eternal torment, of being cast out into Gehenna, of wailing and grinding of teeth. These seem to be two contradictory views of God. The doubt returns—is God in fact indifferent to us?

## Our Freedom to Reject God

God does not want anyone to go to hell, but creates it as a state for those who reject Him, and *want* to be separated from Him. There has to be some accommodation for Hell because God respects our freedom. So if we want to reject Him, reject others, and reject love, then God has to provide some domain in which people who want to spend eternity being like this can do it.

## Hell Is a Place to Be Away from Heaven

Such people certainly cannot do this in the Kingdom of Heaven, which is unconditional love. If God grants us all eternal life, there has to be a place for people who want to reject God, others, and love that can't be the same as the Kingdom of Heaven. They need a place where they can have what they want.

### NOTES

 **GEHENNA**

Originally the name of a valley used by pagan tribes for child sacrifice and hence seen as cursed land, its meaning expanded in the Bible to refer to the place of eternal absence from God, of darkness, and of torment. In this meaning it is synonymous with the modern English "Hell".

 **"WAILING AND GRINDING OF TEETH"**

This unusual biblical phrase is typically found in parables, describing those "cast out" into darkness or Gehenna. "Wailing" is often used in Scripture to indicate lamentation (think of the feeling in English of phrases such as "lamenting his fate" or simply "woe is me!"). Grinding of teeth is used throughout the bible to depict anger. The combination suggests a specific kind of emotion—self-pity and anger—the emotion one might find in someone throwing a tantrum or, more seriously, a person who has closed himself off from any outside love or healing.

 **AUTONOMOUS**

Self-governing, in control of itself, independent, not answerable to anyone.

## The Choice of Isolation

In *The Great Divorce*, C. S. Lewis illustrates the mindset of people who choose Hell by describing Hell as a place where all the houses move further and further away from each other over the years. People get sick and tired of being around other people and all prefer splendid isolation. They can all be completely autonomous; they don't have to listen to anyone, help anyone, or even be with anyone.

They are each king of their own empty domain, forever, just as they want.

# God Welcomes All to Heaven

While people may choose this isolation of Hell, God always welcomes and invites everyone to Heaven. This doesn't mean we need to be perfectly loving when we die. It does mean we have to want to be in an environment where God, others, and love, not only matter, but are of ultimate significance. As Saint Ignatius of Loyola says, even the desire to have the desire will do—such was the attitude of the prodigal son. God can take care of the rest.

**THE GREAT DIVORCE**

(1945) A fantasy written by C. S. Lewis, set on an allegorical bus trip from Hell to the outskirts of Heaven, that explores human choices and how they influence our openness to salvation and happiness.

**NOTES**

God's invitation to salvation is always the same.

Every person has the freedom to open themselves to it or to be alone.

# V. Competing Views of God: The Problem of Evil

Another conflict people perceive with a loving God is why He would allow evil. This is an old and universal question, and it has multiple facets.

**LOVE**
Capacity to see the good news in one another and to enter into an empathetic relationship, where it is just as easy to do the good for the other as it is for ourselves.

*I love you.*

**Free acts can be loving (like this parent holding a kid).**

*I love you.*

**Involuntary acts cannot be loving (like this chair holding a kid).**

## Why Does God Allow Human Evil?

Episode Timecode
**25:38**

### Genuine Love Is Free

Why does God allow people to do evil? As with the problem of Hell, the question comes down to freedom. God gives us the power to love, and genuine love must be free. If you can't choose evil, you can't choose good.

### Robot Love vs. Made in God's Image

The only alternative to freely given love would be forced love. If God didn't allow us to choose evil courses of action, then He would have to program us to do only loving behaviors. We would be like robots with a God chip, programmed to love.

God wants more for us than robotic "love" because we are made in God's image. We are persons; like God we have an intellect to know the truth and a free will to choose the good— to choose love freely, as God loves us freely.

**Saint Ignatius of Loyola**
(1491–1556)
*Priest, theologian*
Founder of the Jesuits, he was the author of the *Spiritual Exercises*, a system of self-examination and prayer that is still widely used today.

## NOTES

# VI. Conclusion

## God's Love Seeks Salvation and Not Punishment

Jesus has revealed that He and the Father love unconditionally and are committed to our salvation. He is not looking to condemn us, and he will never reject us for not being good enough. Like with the prodigal son, the invitation is there no matter what, and we will always be welcomed home.

## Our Freedom and the Problem of Evil

Our love requires freedom. God also has to allow for a domain where people can freely reject him. Jesus tries to warn us that this domain is dark and painful, but He won't force us to come to Him. Amid the presence of evil and love, there is always freedom.

## An Epic Journey toward Transcendence

The choice and the goal both lie before us. God calls us to a relationship of unconditonal love, a transcendent destiny of eternal life, but we are free to choose. We must contend with human and spiritual evil, but through prayer we can draw strength from God. Are you ready to put your faith and trust totally in Him? Are you ready to move into a life of prayer—and a life of virtue?

Are you ready for love? For transcendence? For happiness?

# Lesson Six—Transcendence: Is Unconditional Love Real?

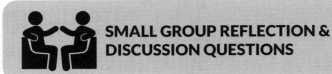

**SMALL GROUP REFLECTION & DISCUSSION QUESTIONS**

1. Is God indifferent to us? What experiences might lead people to think God doesn't care about us? What might lead people to think God does care about us?

2. What has your experience of love been in life? What are your expectations about God's love? How do the two compare?

3. What evidence from near-death experiences indicates the existence of a God of unconditional love? What evidence from the Resurrection of Jesus indicates this?

4. How does the God of unconditional love seem to conflict with the God who speaks of Hell?

5. Why do people need to have freedom in order to love?

6. What happens if you try to force someone to love you? Have you ever experienced someone trying to get love by force?

7. Are you ready to make God and others ultimately significant in your life? Why is that question relevant to your own happiness?

8. What experiences have made you more or less likely to trust in unconditional love? If you choose to trust in God's unconditional love, what would that look like?

**NOTES**

# Lesson Seven—Happiness, Love, and Suffering

## Outline Summary

# I. The Problem of Suffering

In the last lesson, we considered suffering produced by human evil, but another kind of suffering remains: the suffering produced by the forces of nature.

## Why Does God Allow Suffering Caused by Nature?

### Love Incompatible with Suffering?

If God is all-loving, and suffering is incompatible with love, why did he create a natural world that could cause suffering? Why didn't he create us in a perfect world?

### Suffering in Our Culture

This question of suffering weighs on the mind of many people today—this is the issue that leads many in our culture away from God. They can't believe that a God of love would allow suffering, and so they refuse to believe in God. They don't encounter the various kinds of evidence of a loving God, as we have surveyed in the preceding lesson. So when they can't answer the question of suffering, it leads them toward a "cruel God", which incites either indifference to or rejection of him. But there is a crucial flaw in the way they are asking the question—the assumption that love and suffering are incompatible.

**NOTES**

# Lesson Seven—Happiness: Love and Suffering

## What's the Good of Suffering?

### Suffering Can Lead to Love

In fact, most philosophers and theologians believe that suffering can lead to humility, compassion, and virtue.

### Suffering Can Lead to Purpose

Sometimes suffering can snap us out of a superficial life and call us to a deeper reflection about life's purpose. As we know from the four levels of happiness, following our purpose into the higher levels leads to less selfish and more loving behavior.

The time has come to define love a little more clearly.

> ## Suffering Can Lead To:
> - Love
> - Humility
> - Compassion
> - Deeper insight
> - Self-definition
> - Virtue

 **VIRTUE**
An internal and habitual disposition toward good behavior; a standard of moral excellence.

**NOTES**

Episode Timecode
**2:30**

# II. What Is Love? The Four Kinds of Love

In his book *The Four Loves*, C. S. Lewis gives some basic definitions and distinctions for this huge and frequently misunderstood word.

## NOTES

---

### The Four Kinds of Love

- *Storgē*—Affection
- *Filia*—Friendship
- *Eros*—Romance and "First Priority" Relationship
- *Agapē*—Unconditional love for the good of the other alone

 **AGNOSTICISM**

The stance of someone who doesn't know whether or not God exists—this uncertainty may be only personal, or it may be a belief that God's existence is by definition unknowable. Not to be confused with atheism.

 **ATHEISM**

The belief that God definitely does not exist.

# Lesson Seven—Happiness: Love and Suffering

## NOTES

**RECIPROCITY**

A mutual exchange of privileges.

### *Storgē*—Affection

Affection is a natural response to a delightful object. It is primarily emotional. *Storgē* is what is triggered when you encounter a laughing baby or a cute puppy, or the elderly neighbor who always smiles and waves when you pass by at the mailbox. This response may not run very deep, but it is nonetheless a valid form of love.

### *Filia*—Friendship

Friendship is a higher level of love—it runs deeper than the affection we might feel for an acquaintance. What makes a friend more substantial than an acquaintance?

## Reciprocity

Friends are people you appreciate—something about their personality, or their presence makes you want to spend time with them, be loyal to them, be honest around them, and commit yourself to them. But all of this sharing of yourself anticipates a reciprocity—if the other person doesn't feel similarly drawn to you, the friendship will not grow, and it probably won't last long if it even begins.

## Commitment

On the other hand, if the person does reciprocate and shares himself with you, then this mutual sharing engenders a commitment. You become invested in each other and are motivated to give more of yourself, in the expectation that your friend will do the same for you and that the friendship will grow. Really good friends feel that they would do just about anything for each other—they are loyal and committed. Note that this commitment is not exclusive or romantic.

**COMPLEMENTARITY**

A combination of things in a way that brings out the best qualities of each, such that they "complete" each other.

**"FIRST PRIORITY" RELATIONSHIP**

The relationship between two people who are each the most important priority in the other's life.

**NOTES**

# Lesson Seven—Happiness: Love and Suffering

## *Eros*—Romance

 Episode Timecode **4:36**

### Complex and Powerful

Romance is a combination of several strong and interrelated desires. *Eros* refers to more than simply biological sex. Sexuality is one element, as is the fascinating mystery of "the other gender", the attraction of beauty, intimations of marriage and family, and the anticipation which comes from all these elements wrapped up together—an anticipation for the one person with whom you will bond in a "first priority" relationship.

### The "First Priority" Relationship

We want to be the most important priority and relationship in another person's life. This is what *eros* motivates us to seek, and it has built-in characteristics.

### Mutual Exclusivity

Just as friendship requires reciprocity, even more so does a "first priority" relationship. If you are going to ask someone to make you the most important priority in their life, you also have to do the same for them. And since each person can only have one first priority, this means the relationship must be mutually exclusive.

### Sharing the Whole Self

As a result, a mutual "first priority" relationship naturally orients itself toward a person we can share our whole self with: someone who will complement us, someone we can raise children with and grow old with, someone we can trust completely, and someone who will commit to us at the highest level. This complex psychological desire goes far beyond the simple elements, such as physical attraction or a desire for a family, yet these elements are all real and coinvolved in this desire.

NOTES

## "First Priority" Relationship

## Someone We Can:

- Share our whole self with
- Raise children with
- Grow old with
- Trust completely
- Do things with that we can't do by ourself
- Mutually support and complement

## NOTES

## *Agapē*—Unconditional Love

### Love without Reward

The three kinds of love so far involve a giving of oneself to another, and receiving something in return.

*Storgē*—*affection and emotion*

*Filia*—*reciprocity and commitment*

*Eros*—*exclusive commitment and romance*

The final and highest kind of love is ***agapē***. *Agapē* is completely unselfish, focusing only on the goodness and value it sees in the other person in himself. It requires no reward.

### "Greater Love Hath No Man . . ." —The Power of *Agapē* in the World

Many of the most valued expressions of love in our world come from *agapē*.

*Agapē* is the only kind of love that can initiate forgiveness, compassion for the marginalized, and sympathy for the sick. These are acts of love that don't come with a reward attached to them.

You can see why Jesus established *agapē* as the highest kind of love. It is the love that can embrace the prodigal son with open arms and welcome him into the heavenly banquet.

---

 **SELF-DEFINITION**

Defining our character by our actions and choices.

## The Four Levels of Love and Suffering

What we believe about happiness will determine how we define five other important concepts—love, suffering, freedom, ethics, and the common good. Just as there are four levels of happiness, so also there are four levels of these other concepts. The concept we are interested in here is "love".

People on happiness Level 1 generally view love as the satisfaction of physical-sexual desires. People on happiness Level 2 view love as being loved and admired by others. People on Level 3 view love as contributing to, caring for, and attending to others—and working with others for a common good. On Level 4, love has the same characteristics as Level 3 but goes beyond *this* world—so it is contributing to, caring for, and attending to others' faith, hope, salvation, and transcendent dignity and mystery.

Notice that *storgē* is possible on all four levels of love, because it is only a feeling. However, it is very difficult—if not impossible—to have meaningful *filia* (friendships), meaningful *eros* ("first priority" friendship and commitment), and *agapē* (self-sacrificial love for the good of the other alone) on Levels 1 and 2. These three kinds of love are available only for people living on Levels 3 or 4. If someone is living on Level 4, he will infuse his *filia*, *eros*, and *agapē* with concern for the other person's eternal destiny, transcendent dignity, and salvation.

We are now in a position to see how love and suffering can be compatible. As you can imagine, suffering and love are completely incompatible for people who are dominant Level 1 or Level 2. Suffering can't possibly fulfill someone's physical-sexual desires (Level 1) or one's desire to be loved and admired by others (Level 2). However, suffering can have an essential positive influence on Level 3 love, because it can help people to seek deeper meaning in life, humility, courage, virtue, compassion, and care for others. Furthermore, the suffering of others creates the opportunity for us to respond to them with care, compassion, humility, and courage. Similarly, suffering helps people living on Level 4 to trust radically in God, seek their eternal destiny and transcendent dignity as their first priority, and seek God's grace through prayer. This trust, grace, and transcendent perspective enhance and fortify our unselfish care for and compassion toward other human beings in their transcendent dignity.

It is here that the example of Jesus Christ on the Cross comes fully into play. Even though Jesus' act of complete self-sacrifice looks like a meaningless and ignominious death to people living on Levels 1 and 2, it manifests complete self-sacrificial love to those living on Level 3. For those living on Level 4, Jesus offers his life as an act of love for the *salvation* of the whole *world*. We can offer up our suffering to the Father in the same way with the same intention to help others in their salvation.

### *Agapē* Is the Only Kind of Love That Can Initiate:

- Forgiveness
- Compassion for the marginalized
- Sympathy for the sick

**NOTES**

## NOTES

 Episode Timecode
**9:30**

# III. Suffering and Purpose

## Suffering and the Pursuit of Happiness

In fact, there are many ways suffering can contribute to our pursuit of happiness.

## Overcoming Superficiality

Suffering can redirect our attention when we are living a superficial life, snapping us out of our distractions and complacency and forcing us to look—perhaps for the first time—at the deeper purpose of our lives.

## Escaping Narcissism

We encountered narcissism in the Comparison Game. Looking down on other people, thinking we are the best, withdrawing into ourselves— suffering can shatter all these illusions by forcing us to accept, in our difficulties, that we need the support of others. This orientation toward others sets us on the path to a contributive life, moving us into the higher levels of happiness.

## Defining Character

Suffering confronts us with challenges, and our responses to those challenges develop and define our character. Consider these examples:

- **Courage**

  We can never know if we are courageous unless we experience fear, and fear presumes suffering.

- **Compassion**

  If the world were perfect, no one would need us or our compassion— and we wouldn't need anybody or their compassion either. We would never know if we were capable of compassion or *agapē*.

# Lesson Seven—Happiness: Love and Suffering

## Improving the World

In fact, had God placed us in a perfect world, there would be nothing for us to do, no way of improving the world, no way of getting together with other human beings for a common cause.

## "There Are Worse Things Than Suffering"

Father Spitzer recalls this expression of his father. It would be worse to live a life without courage, self-sacrifice for a noble cause, compassion, and self-definition.

### A Life of Pleasure

He paints a picture of a life in which we are sheltered from all difficulties: just born into a pleasure bubble and drifting through life being coddled by God like little babies.

### A Life of Growth

This thought reveals that growth in life requires suffering and leads us to our highest qualities and purpose: courage, nobility, making a difference in the world and joining with others to build the Kingdom of God.

## Aids to Suffering

- Spontaneous prayers
- Looking for the good
- Following the Holy Spirit

**NOTES**

Episode Timecode
**18:45**

## Case Study: John Chavez

At age 24, this young lifeguard expected he had reached the point in his life where he would find the right woman and get married and start a family. Instead, he went into the hospital one day for a routine operation but, due to complications, found himself permanently blind.

At this catastrophic disruption of his life, John Chavez was faced with a choice: to go down the path of despair for the life-style he had lost, or to move forward down the path of faith to see what new life was now in store for him.

He was confronted with this choice as soon as he got out of the hospital. The head trauma rehab center rejected him—incredibly, on the grounds that he was blind. Their program didn't have accommodations for the blind and couldn't take him. John said he was coming anyway—he needed the program, and they'd just have to figure something out.

By the time he left, the center had four other blind students.

Where does the motivation come from to go down the path of faith and keep trying things in the face of setbacks? John says anyone can do it, but we often don't, because we look at what we can't do instead of what we can do. We put God in a box and say there's only one way, but John observes that God is infinite and has other ways for us.

When his own plans fell through, he kept his faith that God would take care of him in his own way and following his own timetable.

He has been led to new people, new challenges, new accomplishments, new relationships, and new memories on the path God led him down after he lost his sight. In fact, he's getting married to the love of his life, 30 years later than he had once expected to marry and under circumstances he never would have anticipated.

And he couldn't be happier.

### NOTES

## "There are worse things than suffering."

### NOTES

### How to Suffer Well

Episode Timecode
**24:59**

If we know that suffering is part of our journey to happiness, we can move beyond just "trying to get through it," to finding ways to suffer well and make our lives better in the process.

### Spontaneous Prayer

Turning to God in the moment we experience suffering allows us to obtain God's assistance, most importantly, but it also helps remind us to see the suffering from a higher perspective.

### Looking for the Good

As we have seen, suffering can lead us to deeper insight and give us opportunities to improve ourselves through self-definition and self-sacrifice. Looking for these opportunities in the suffering we encounter gives us something positive to focus on and even appreciate.

### Following the Holy Spirit

"When one door slams, the Spirit opens another"—we should remember, when we encounter difficulties, that setbacks sometimes allow the Spirit to force us off the path we were contentedly on, and to look around to discover the greater path God has in store for us.

## "When one door slams, the Spirit opens another."

**Happiness is a complex issue.**

We've come through the **four levels of happiness**.

We've seen the **need to move** to Levels 3 and 4

and to look for the **good news** in others.

We've also seen how faith can lead to a much **broader and richer life**.

We looked at the evidence for **God**, our **soul**, and **life after death**.

We looked at the **unconditional love** of God,

the inevitability of **evil**, and

the mystery of **suffering**.

## NOTES

Episode Timecode
**36:29**

# IV. Conclusion

Through it all, we've seen how happiness, love, freedom, suffering, and faith are connected.

When they are all put together, they express our true dignity and destiny in the unconditionally loving God—the one who helps us through the struggles of superficiality, misuses of freedom, and imperfections in ourselves and others, and who guides us on our way to greater love through His Son, Jesus.

Saint Augustine said, "For you have made us for Yourself, and our hearts are restless until they rest in You."

**So now we leave you with this final challenge:**

- What are the steps you want to take to satisfy the restless heart?

- How will you move into the fullness of love, faith, freedom, happiness, and life?

- What will you do to bring yourself closer to the unconditionally loving God?

Thank you for joining us on this journey
into the heights of happiness.

# Lesson Seven—Happiness: Love and Suffering

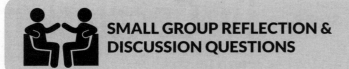 **SMALL GROUP REFLECTION & DISCUSSION QUESTIONS**

1. Why would an all-loving God allow suffering and evil caused by nature?

2. Why didn't God create us in a perfect world?

3. Can you give examples from your life of each of the four loves?

4. Have you ever been improved by a painful experience? Have you had a painful experience that left you worse off? What caused the difference?

5. When has someone shown love for you through suffering?

6. When have you shown someone love through suffering? What was the result?

7. Have you ever faced a loss or obstacle that caused great suffering in the moment, but that set you on the path to receive a greater good later, which you might have otherwise missed?

8. What does suffering have to do with your happiness?

9. What does love have to do with your happiness?

10. The soul, the Resurrection, faith in a God of unconditional love—are these significant in a journey to a transcendent life? Why or why not?

11. What has changed for you through the study of happiness?

12. What are you going to do now?

**NOTES**

# About the Author: Father Robert J. Spitzer, S.J., Ph.D.

Born in Honolulu, Hawaii, on May 16, 1952, Father Spitzer is a Catholic priest in the Jesuit order, and is currently the President of the Magis Center of Reason and Faith (www.magiscenter.com) and the Spitzer Center (www.spitzercenter.org). The Magis Center produces documentaries, books, high school curricula, college courses, adult-education curricula, and new-media materials to show the close connection between faith and reason in contemporary astrophysics, philosophy, and historical study of the New Testament. The Spitzer Center produces facilitated curricula to strengthen culture, faith, and spirit in Catholic organizations as well as nonprofit and for-profit organizations.

Father Spitzer was President of Gonzaga University from 1998 to 2009. He has made multiple media appearances including Larry King Live (debating Stephen Hawking, Deepak Chopra, and Leonard Mlodinow about creation and science), the Today Show, the History Channel in "God and the Universe", and a multiple-part PBS series "Closer to the Truth". He has also appeared on dozens of nationally syndicated radio programs. He has given hundreds of presentations to universities, learned societies, professional societies, corporations, nonprofit organizations, and government agencies both nationally and internationally (including members of Tony Blair's Cabinet in London, officials of the Russian Orthodox Church in Russia, both sides of the conflict in Northern Ireland, government officials in El Salvador, as well as international universities, corporations, and Catholic organizations).

Robert J. Spitzer, S.J., Ph.D.

Happiness! The Series addresses the most basic but often un-examined question of happiness—what it is, where it comes from, and how it defines the choices in our lives.

This companion Study Guide outlines the key points from each of the seven episodes in the series and provides supplemental information and review tools to help you engage the questions raised and ponder their implications for your own life today.

Each chapter includes

- Biographies of great thinkers and contemporary figures referenced in the series
- Discussion questions and exercises
- Quotations for reflection
- Definitions of key terms
- Diagrams and illustrations
- Workbook space for notes

## Other Books by Father Spitzer

*Finding True Happiness: Satisfying Our Restless Hearts*

*New Proofs for the Existence of God:*
*Contributions of Contemporary Physics and Philosophy*
(Winner of the Catholic Press Association Award
for best book in faith and science)

*Ten Universal Principles: A Brief Philosophy of the Life Issues*

*Healing the Culture: A Commonsense Philosophy of Happiness, Freedom, and the Life Issues*

*Spirit of Leadership:*
*Optimizing Creativity and Change in Organizations*

*Five Pillars of the Spiritual Life:*
*A Practical Guide to Prayer for Active People*

# Image Credits

Jeffrey Mitchell: 1, 17, 35, 52, 71, 83.

Katherine Turner: 7, 11, 18, 32, 40, 50, 54, 58, 79, 80, 86, 88, 89.

## Other sources: